# If I Ran the
# Horse Show

IF I RAN THE HORSE SHOW
A BANTAM BOOK 978 0 857 51359 5

First published in Great Britain by Bantam,
an imprint of Random House Children's Publishers UK
A Random House Group Company

This edition published 2013


TM and © by Dr. Seuss Enterprises, L.P. 2013 Published by arrangement with Random House
Children's Books U.S., a division of Random House, Inc.


THE CAT IN THE HAT KNOWS A LOT ABOUT THAT! logo and word mark TM 2010
Dr. Seuss Enterprises, L.P., and Portfolio Entertainment Inc., and
Collingwood O'Hare Productions, Ltd.

Bantam Books are published by Random House Children's Publishers UK,
61–63 Uxbridge Road, London W5 5SA

www.randomhousechildrens.co.uk
www.randomhouse.co.uk

Addresses for companies within The Random House Group Limited can be found at: www.
randomhouse.co.uk/offices.htm


THE RANDOM HOUSE GROUP Limited Reg. No. 954009

A CIP catalogue record for this book is available from the British Library.

Printed in China

# If I Ran the Horse Show

by Bonnie Worth

illustrated by Aristides Ruiz and Joe Mathieu

BANTAM BOOKS

I'm the Cat in the Hat!
And today we will go
to my Super-Tremendous
Stupendous Horse Show!

But I warn you, I might
get a little bit sappy.
When it comes to horses,
I get really happy!

SUPER-
TREMENDOUS
STUPENDOUS
HORSE SHOW

Horses and people
have long worked as one.
They've formed a strong bond,
when all's said and done.

Horses were hunted
by cavemen as prey.

Farmers learned later
to make them obey.

All horses are treated
(you will find this fact fun)
as if they were born
on January one.

JAN.
1

A foal is a horse who
is less than one year.
A yearling (surprise!)
is a year – is that clear?

MARE/DAM

FOAL

A filly's a female
who is less than four.
A mare is a female
who's four years or more.

A colt is a male horse
who is less than four.
A stallion's a male
who's four years or more.

A dam is a horse
who is also a mama.
A sire is a stallion,
a horse's papa.

STALLION/SIRE

YEARLING

*Gelding* is the word
that people use for
a male who can't
make foals anymore.

GELDING

Before we go on,
it is good, I suppose,
to look at a horse
from its tail to its nose.

The top of the tail is
what we call the dock.
Then haunch and stifle
and gaskin and hock.
Hip, loins, back, flank,
withers, poll, crest.

Now take a deep breath
and go on with the rest.
Neck, jaw, and chin groove,
forehead and foretop,
nostril and muzzle – is
it time to stop?

LOIN

POINT
of HIP

HAUNCH

DOCK

FLANK

STIFLE

GASKIN

CANNON

HOCK

PASTERN

FETLOCK

HOOF

POLL    FORETOP

CREST

NECK    FOREHEAD

MUZZLE

NOSTRIL

WITHERS

JAW

BACK

CHIN GROOVE

POINT of SHOULDER

CHEST

FOREARM

ELBOW

No! Our look at the horse
can't be rated complete
until we have looked at
the legs and the feet.

KNEE

Hoof, coronet, pastern,
knee and fetlock,

CORONET    elbow and cannon,

Nerves under horsehide
can feel a fly creeping.
A tail fends off flies
by swatting and sweeping.

RIGHT EYE

OTH
YES

LEFT EYE

Eyes set on the side,

as with all those that are prey,
see predators coming
from far, far away.

Legs made for running
help horses to hie.
Flat hooves keep them steady
on wet turf or dry.

Most horses we ride –
this will not be big news –
have hooves that are guarded
by strong iron shoes.

Horse hooves, like your nails,
are made up of stuff
that doesn't have feeling.
Oh, hoof stuff is tough!

A farrier trims horses' hooves
with a file.
Horses should have this done
every once in a while.

He heats up horseshoes
until they are hot,
then nails them on tight.
Does it hurt? It does not!

Horses step out, or move,
at a number of rates.

Walk,  trot,

canter, gallop –

we call these steps gaits.

Standardbred horses
can move at a pace,
a fast gait they use
when they run in a race.

The Icelandic pony
has what's called a tolt,
a swift gait that's smooth,
with nary a jolt.

Both Standard and Icy,
these two that you see,
are what we call breeds.
What are breeds? you ask me.

They are horses who mix
with similar mates
and give birth to foals
who have the same traits.

This breed is a Clydesdale.
It's bred to be big.
The Falabella is as small
as a six-month-old pig.

The Clydesdale, we know,
measures eighteen hands high.
The Falabella is seven.
What a cute little guy!

A hand is four inches.
It equals the span
of a hand that belongs
to a fully grown man.

We start from the ground
and then measure till we
get up to the withers –
no higher. You see?

Quarter horse is a breed
that started out West.
It's easy to handle and
herds cows the best.

Appaloosas are horses
that are covered with spots.
Native Americans liked
this spotted breed lots.

In the sandy Sahara
the Arabian's a prize.
It has grace and speed
and a delicate size.

It can do with less water
in dry desert lands
and runs without sinking
deep into desert sands.

Arabians now live
the whole world round.
Where there are horse lovers,
this breed can be found.

With large eyes and nostrils
and a dainty muzzle,
it's easy to handle
and happy to nuzzle.

The Fjord (FEE-ord), from Norway,
can deal with rough weather.
They say it is stronger
than good, tough shoe leather.

Australian stock horses –
sometimes called Walers –
came Down Under with British
settlers and sailors.

Connemara ponies go
on great riding tours
of Ireland's fair marshes
and its rolling moors.

These hunters and jumpers –
so the story goes –
swam from Spanish shipwrecks.
But who really knows!

Answer this question
and you'll win a prize.
Is being a pony
a matter of size?

A grown horse that's less
than fourteen hands, two
you say is a pony.

16

14

13

12

11

The Lipizzan horse
from the Spanish Riding School
can dance and prance nimbly –
so elegant and cool!

A Lipizzan's proud,
with a beautiful mane,
crossbred from Arabians
and horses from Spain.

The school is in Austria
and has won worldwide fame.
Its half-Spanish horses
inspired the school's name.

The Morgan is smart
and learns quickly how
to pull rigs, plow the fields,
run a race, herd a cow.

Thoroughbred is a horse
born and bred for the track.
It carries a jockey
upon its sleek back.

It runs in big races
of worldwide renown
like the Ascot, the Epsom,
and the Triple Crown.

Mustangs roam wild
on the wide-open plains.
They've never known saddles
or the feel of the reins.

Bit, reins, and saddle
are what we call tack.
Reins and bit on the head,
saddle over the back.

BIT

HEADSTALL

HORN

CANTLE

POMMEL

JOCKEY

REAR
JOCKEY

CHIN
STRAP

SEAT

GULLET

REINS

LATIGO
KEEPER

LATIGO

SKIRT

CINCH
RING

STIRRUP
LEATHER

STIRRUP

CINCH

WESTERN

There are western saddles
and the English kind.
The difference between them
let us bear in mind.

BROWBAND

HEADSTALL

CHEEK PIECE

NOSEBAND

THROATLATCH

CANTLE

POMMEL

GULLET

SEAT

REINS

BIT

FLAP

GIRTH

LEATHERS

STIRRUP IRON

ENGLISH

Western is made
for the cowboy's long haul.

English is for hunting and
jumping and all.

On English, we post
and we must learn the knack
of rising up off of
the trotting horse back.

We stick to the western
and we do not rise.
Either English or western
is great exercise!

Now put on the saddle,
the reins, and the bit.
Your hard riding cap –
you can't forget it!

The judges are waiting.

It's time for the show.

So pick up the reins . . .

. . . giddyup and let's go!

# GLOSSARY

**Down Under:** A term used for Australia, which is "down under" the equator.

**Farrier:** A person trained to put shoes on horses.

**Hie:** To go quickly.

**Inspired:** Filled with the spirit to do something.

**Jockey:** A person who rides a racehorse.

**Knack:** A special ability.

**Moor:** Grassy, wind-swept land with few trees.

**Nary a:** Another way of saying "not one."

**Nimbly:** Lightly and quickly.

**Post:** To rise and fall with the movement of a trotting horse.

**Predator:** A hunter.

**Prey:** An animal that is hunted.

**Trait:** An inherited quality.